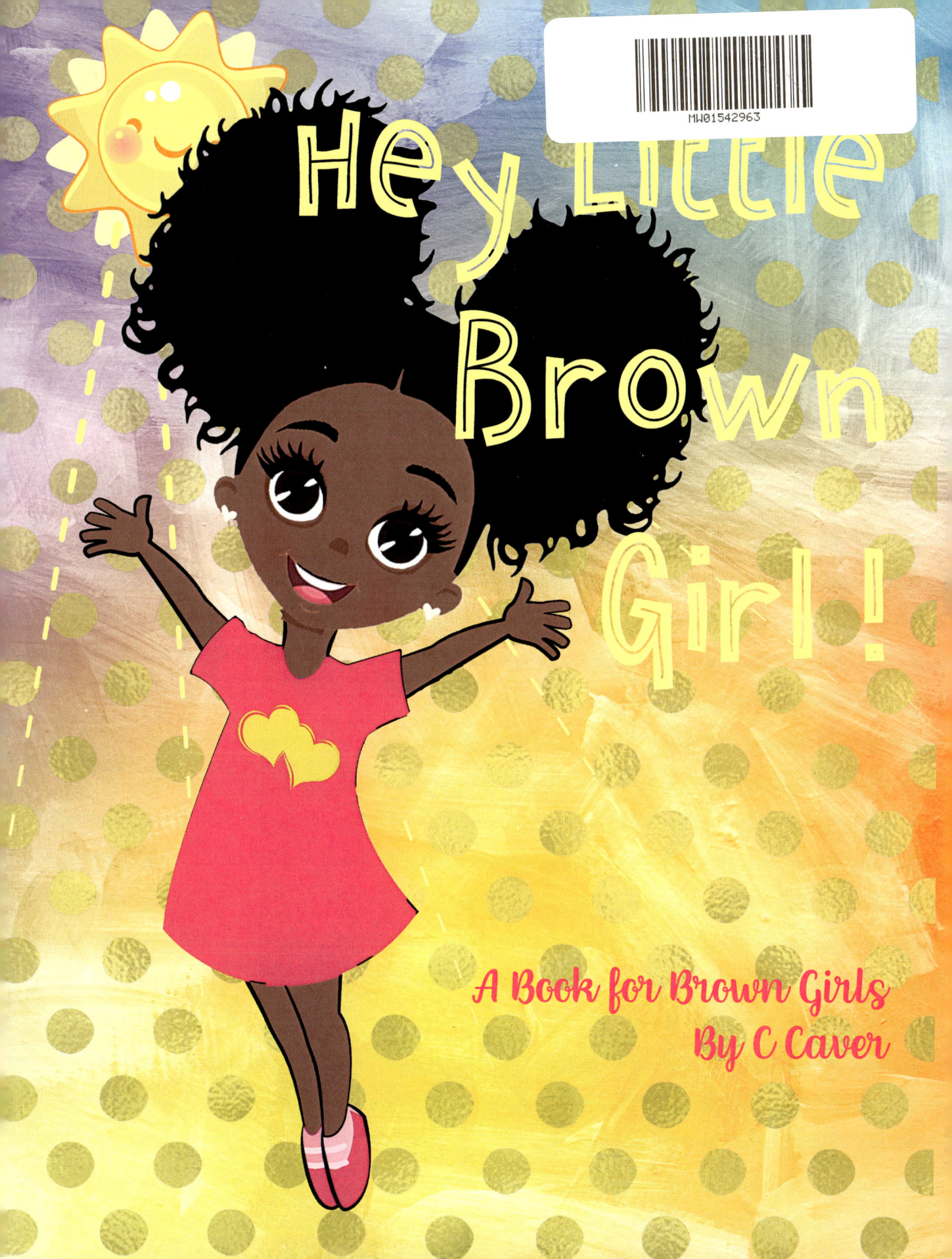

Look at your skin, eyes, nose and hair.
You are uniquely made that's why we all love to stop and stare.

Wow, look at your smile! You're standing so tall and shining so bright.

Just like the stars gleaming at night.

Amazing,
Awesome,
and
Brilliant!
That's what
I see.

Your spirit is pure and your heart is loving.

that's the key!

when you're around you light up the room. wow look at that GLOW

You are confident, funny, kind and loving too.

Everyone would be happy to have a friend just like you!

You always make me laugh. You are such a great friend to me!

You know your colors, numbers, letters, and draw the best pictures when it's time for art!

That's how I know you are filled with so much love

I have to say it out loud.

Little Brown Girl, YOU ARE THE BEST!

Hey Little Brown Girl

By C. Caver

First, Thank you... Thank you for picking up this book. This book was written and illustrated with tons of love. My mom and sister edited my writing. My daughter gave input on the colors and illustrations, and my sons helped entertain their younger siblings so I could finally complete this book.

When you have a purpose. God will gather the troops to fulfill the mission. So as you read this book, Rather you have daughter, or a student in your class that needs a reminder of how amazing she is. know we are all apart of the mission. Uplifting and building the confidence of our little brown girls.

Please don't hesitate to email me cc@justaskcc.com